WILDLIFE WATCHER'S

ACADIA

NATIONAL PARK

By Ruth Gortner Grierson

NORTHWORD
PRESS, INC

Minocqua, Wisconsin

To my father, Charles F. Gortner, Jr., from whom I inherited my joy of writing, and to my children, Heather and Scott, with whom I share a great love for the natural world

My special thanks to the following for their invaluable review of the text. My good friend, Heidi Welch, naturalist; my daughter, Heather Grierson, Curator of Animals at the Acadia Zoo in Trenton, Maine; and my son, Scott Grierson, Nature Educator for Friends of Acadia.

I also appreciate the generous gift of time given in editing the manuscript from good friends James Gower and Mardie Junkins.

I recognize, too, the dedicated park naturalists who work tirelessly to assist visitors and residents on MDI in learning about the natural wonders of Acadia National Park.

Photography © 1995:
   Cover, 25, 31, 44-45, 48, 54, 56, 57, 61, 62, 67, 69, 70, 78 (bottom), 82, 83, 86 (both), 89—The Wildlife Collection; Cover (light house inset), 1 (light house inset), 3, 10-11, 15, 22, 28, 36, 40, 41, 51, 59, 65, 77, 87, 90-91, 95,—Dembinsky Photo Associates;   1, 16-17, 32, 35, 38, 46, 80 (top), 81, 88—Susan Winton/Aurora;   5, 20-21—Stephen J. Krasemann;   6, 79—John Hendrickson;   27—John Netherton;   52, 74-75, 76, 84—Richard Hamilton Smith;   43, 63, 78 (top), 85—Bruce Coleman, Inc.;   24, 39, 73, 80 (bottom), back cover—Robert W. Baldwin

Cover design by Russell S. Kuepper
Book design by Kenneth A. Hey

NorthWord Press, Inc.
P.O. Box 1360 / Minocqua, WI 54548

For a free catalog describing NorthWord's line of books and gift items, call toll free 1-800-336-5666

Printed in Hong Kong

Library of Congress Cataloging-in-Publication Data
Grierson, Ruth Gortner.
      Acadia National Park: wildlife watcher's guide / by Ruth Gortner Grierson.
      Includes bibliographical references.
      ISBN 1-55971-455-7
      1. Wildlife watching—Maine—Acadia National Park—Guidebooks. 2. Wildlife viewing sites—Maine—Acadia National Park—Guidebooks. 3. Zoology—Maine—Acadia National Park. 4. Acadia National Park (Me.)—Guidebooks. I. Title
      QL181.G74 1995   94-40926
      599.09741'45—dc20   CIP

ABOUT THIS GUIDE

Acadia National Park: A Wildlife Watcher's Guide is designed to make your search for mammals and birds within Acadia National Park as simple as possible. From tiny warblers to huge whales, from eagles to a bull moose this book can be your companion for finding the best viewing spots for the park's wildlife.

The guide offers helpful tips for finding and observing wildlife as well as intimate life histories of the fascinating birds and mammals to be seen in the park. By using narratives, color photographs, maps, charts, and specific recommendations concerning where to travel, your explorations in the only national park in the northeast will be very rewarding.

Contents

ACADIA NATIONAL PARK

Belfast

Ellsworth

Schoodic Peninsula

Mount Desert Island

Isle au Haut

- National Park
- Loons
- Mergansers
- Cormorants
- Deer
- Eagles
- Eiders
- Great Blue Herons
- Hawks
- Moose
- Osprey
- Peregrines
- Ravens
- Seals
- Sandpipers
- Ring-Billed Gulls
- Warblers
- — Road

Acadia National Park

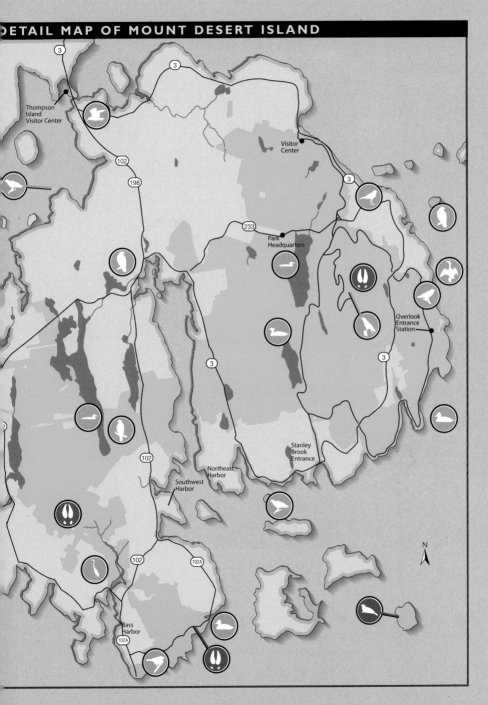

Thompson Island Visitor Center

Visitor Center

Park Headquarters

Overlook Entrance Station

Stanley Brook Entrance

Northeast Harbor

Southwest Harbor

Bass Harbor

N

9

INTRODUCTION

When talking about Acadia National Park it is impossible not to talk about the whole of Mount Desert Island (MDI). This 10,800 square mile island is thirteen miles wide and is partially divided by Somes Sound, the only fjord on the Atlantic coast of the United States. The park is quite spread out, with parcels of land on both sides of MDI as well as on the mainland several miles away. The only formal entrance or exit is found as

you come on and off the island at the Trenton Bridge, a few miles outside of Ellsworth, Maine, on Route 3. It would be wonderful if the whole island were a national park, but private residences were here long before the park was established, so it is a shared habitat.

The park boundaries are irregular, especially on the western side of the island. The Visitor Center is in Hulls Cove on Route 3, where the Park Loop

Road starts. Access to this road can also be made at other locations. The only toll road is a special one-way stretch of the Park Loop Road starting near Sieur de Monts Spring. This eleven mile long, one-way stretch is often referred to as the Ocean Drive and is very scenic. You can stop anywhere on the right for viewing and photographing, and you can park in designated areas for easy access to excellent hiking trails. Sand Beach is on this part of the Park Loop Road and is a popular place for the hardy souls who enjoy swimming or playing in frigid waters. It is the only sandy beach on the island.

A portion of the park is on the Schoodic Peninsula near Winter Harbor, Maine, and although close as a crow flies, it is about 45 miles by car from Bar Harbor. Sightings of sea birds are plentiful in this part of the park making it well worth the trip. The other remote part of the park is on Isle au Haut, 60 miles from Bar Harbor down the coast. It is accessible by ferry and a good place to observe birds, especially osprey and sea ducks.

Most of the more than 120 miles of hiking trails in Acadia National Park are on the eastern side of Mount Desert Island. Excellent trail maps are available at the Visitor Center. These trails range from very easy to strenuous. The carriage road system makes it possible to roam easily on foot or by bicycle for more than 55 miles. (This network of roads was financed and the building directed by John D. Rockefeller, Jr., between 1915 and 1933.) Some carriage roads are open to horses, which can be rented at Wildwood Stables in the park. By walking in the woods on trails and carriage roads you will have the best chance of seeing wildlife and really get to experience a Maine woods. Always stay on the trails and carriage roads so the wildlife habitat is not disturbed.

Acadia can be enjoyed year-round and the birds and mammals to be seen will vary by season. For instance, the possibility of seeing avian visitors such as snowy owls, rough-legged hawks, great gray owls, king eiders and others from the far north and the Arctic makes braving a Maine winter worth the effort. Please note that only the Blackwoods campground near Bar Harbor is open year-round. The campground at Seawall on the western side of MDI is not open in the winter.

Land and sea meet in Acadia, and northern and temperate zones also meet and overlap. This makes it a paradise for bird watchers. You can see some 300 species of birds here, 122 of which are breeding species. Fall migration adds some interesting birds, and storms at sea sometimes push odd species into view along the shores.

Whether you explore Acadia National Park by car, horse, bicycle or foot, you will find it a special place.

TIPS FOR WILDLIFE WATCHERS

Acadia National Park is located on Mount Desert Island off the coast of Maine: It is one of nature's jewels in a magnificent setting. Not only are there mammals and birds living here but a host of other creatures also share this habitat. Five species of snakes and three species of turtles can be found in this region as well as six species of frogs and six species of salamanders. A great many varieties of butterflies and moths are also seen in the area.

The intertidal life along the rocky shoreline adds even more interesting forms of wildlife. Tide pools are miniature marine environments often filled with fascinating creatures and plants, as well as both fresh- and saltwater fish.

The area is a delight to botanists and those who love wildflowers. There are possibly as many as 1,500 species of plants found in Acadia. A great variety of trees and shrubs also make the park's forests special places to explore.

It is also an area of great interest to geologists. The oldest rocks in Acadia, called the Ellsworth Formation, are located just as you come onto the island. They were laid down some 460 million years ago and are composed of thinly layered sediments of silt, sand, mud and volcanic ash which have been highly contorted by the heat and pressure of later land movements. A bold set of flat strata called the Bar Harbor Series is found on the Porcupine Islands and Bar Island in Bar Harbor. These great slabs of granite are enjoyed by hikers on the shores and mountains.

The National Park has available a very helpful checklist of birds in the park—a must for bird watchers.

There are no guarantees in wildlife watching but there are some things you can do to improve your chances of success:

• Use binoculars and a telephoto camera lens to get closer looks at wild creatures without disturbing them.

• Use your car as a blind. Wildlife will often be completely unconcerned about your presence if you stay in the car and talk softly, if at all.

• Wear clothes that blend in with your surroundings.

• Walk quietly and leave your pet at home. Even a well behaved pet will make wildlife nervous at best and usually will make wildlife disappear.

• Use your ears in finding wildlife. If you are camping do not always have the radio or TV turned on. Listen to the wild sounds around you.

• Check out a territory in the daylight and then go back at night with your flashlight and listen to the night sounds, especially on the carriage roads. Be as quiet as you can.

• Sit quietly in one spot and wait for the birds and mammals to come to you. Don't be in a hurry to see wildlife.

A WILDLIFE WATCHER'S CODE OF CONDUCT

A wonderful saying I've heard many times expresses a good philosophy for visitors to the park: "Leave nothing but footprints; take nothing but pictures and memories." To that end the following advice will make your stay a fruitful and happy one.

Stay on the trails

Because of the heavy use of the carriage roads in July and August, wildlife encounters are best experienced in the early morning and late in the day.

Official park maps are available at the Visitor Center on Route 3 and are good guides for trail locations. Be aware that many park roads are closed to vehicle traffic during the winter season.

Build a safe campfire

Many visitors to Acadia enjoy camping in the area, to better their chances of seeing some of the rare wildlife. Always be careful with campfires, and build them only in designated areas.

Drive slowly

Many of the wildlife species in the area are easily startled by automobiles. Be sure to watch carefully for unexpected wildlife along the roadway.

Respect wildlife

Don't get too close; it can put undue stress on wild creatures. A good way to get a closer look is to use binoculars or a spotting scope. Cameras with telephoto lenses are also popular for the many photo opportunities.

Move slowly and casually, not directly at wildlife. Allow them to keep you in view. Do not sneak up and surprise them. Never touch or try to rescue an animal found by itself. Report any real emergency to a ranger.

Restrain Your Pets

Keep pets on a leash at all times while you are in the park and keep your dog from barking unnecessarily. A barking dog can spoil any chances of seeing wildlife for you and others. Letting your dog run freely even if it is well behaved may seem all right but it is not being considerate of the local wildlife and other visitors to the park. It is also illegal.

Never feed the animals

Do not feed wild animals in the park. This includes not leaving trash and food in picnic areas, which may be harmful to the the wildlife. As a visitor in the wildlife's home, enjoy the beauty of the park and be considerate of all its wild inhabitants.

NATURE CRUISES

Unique to Acadia National Park is the availability of watching wildlife while cruising on the local waters surrounding the park. Tour boats leave from Bar Harbor, Northeast Harbor, Southwest Harbor and Bass Harbor. Trips are available throughout the day, seven days a week from several operators.

Right from the moment you board one of these vessels your adventure begins—the harbors are good locations in which to see many wild birds, including cormorants and the various local gulls. Ravens, crows and eagles often feed near the mudflats at low tide. Shorebirds, great blue herons, loons and a few species of ducks spend time in the harbors and are frequently viewed at close range as the boats leave these sheltered waters. The birds have become quite accustomed to the comings and goings of all the boats, both large and small, and will continue their activities uninterrupted as you pass. Also, if there is a run of mackerel in a harbor, large flocks of noisy, screaming terns gather to feed on the fish. This can be an exciting sight to witness.

Once the boats have left the harbors, it is quite common to see eagles flying by, sitting atop some large rock, or perched in the trees of the small nearby islands in Frenchman Bay. An eagle's nest is clearly visible on one of the Porcupine Islands.

Boats out of Bar Harbor usually pass by a small island called the Thrumcap, where cormorants are often visible while they rest or stand on the rocks with wings stretched out to dry.

Guillemots and eiders often fly up as the boats move along. Naturalists on these cruises point out the wildlife and answer questions. As you proceed out to sea, away from MDI, and out beyond the many islands dotting the waters around the park, the excitement mounts for wildlife watchers of all ages, because in the deep, far out waters you may see other unusual sea birds, interesting fish or even some whales.

Out about 20 miles, around Mount Desert Rock, a tiny island on which an automated lighthouse is located, a special bird to look for is the greater shearwater. Shearwaters are generally dark above and white below. The greater shearwater has a black bill, and its black cap is sharply defined against a white throat. This large gull-like bird floats high on the water in small flocks and is often seen in this area. On a calm sea they appear like decoys floating peacefully on the water. Skimming over the waves on their stiff wings they will remind you of feathered gliders.

Although rarely seen from shore, gannets are often visible out on the open saltwater, a few miles from land. It is fun to watch these goose-sized birds, with their long wings tipped with black, fly in wide circles over the ocean then rise and plunge into the sea for fish. Gannets appear pointed at both ends because of their pointed bills and pointed tails. Gulls on the other hand have fan-shaped tails.

The day may not be clear and sunny on the water but do not be discouraged, for on foggy days you will have a better chance of seeing the small gray birds called petrels. These little birds spend all of their lives at sea either on or over the water; they only go to land to nest. Foggy weather brings the tiny fish they eat close to the surface where they are then snatched up by the petrels. The flight of a petrel is reminiscent of a tree swallow dipping and diving over a pond.

A gray day may also make you more attentive to the actual water through which you are moving. The foggy world tends to make you focus on what is nearby and it is at such times you may see the fin of the ocean sun fish, swimming in the waters around the boat. If the word sunfish conjures up a small freshwater fish you may have caught in some small pond, think again, for the ocean sunfish is a very large creature, averaging 5 feet long and weighing as much as 500 pounds. It is said that one can grow to 11 feet and 2,000 pounds! Its grayish skin is thick and tough, the bones soft and weak and its eye quite small in comparison to its body size. This odd fish swimming along in the ocean eats small marine invertebrates and it's always an exciting event if you are lucky enough to see one.

One of the most common reasons wildlife watchers go on nature cruises is to see whales—the largest mammals to be seen in the area of Acadia National Park. In the Gulf of Maine you may see minke, humpback, finback and right whales. Also visible are harbor porpoise, white-sided and white-beaked dolphins. If you're lucky killer whales and pilot whales will present themselves. It is quite possible to go out many times and not see even one of these magnificent mammals of the ocean. But remember, it's also just as possible to go out once and have the thrill of a lifetime with spectacular sightings.

No trip on the water will be wasted for you if you enjoy the varying moods of the ocean and whatever wildlife presents itself on your day at sea.

WILDLIFE ENCOUNTERS

The following chart will help you estimate the likelihood of seeing various species on your visit to Acadia National Park.

■ **Common** On any given day, you should see this species.

◪ **Irregular** The species is not as common, and you must try a little harder to find it.

☐ **Rare** It's still possible to find the species if you use the suggestions given in this book, and have a little luck.

MAMMALS

Beaver	■	Mink	◪	Snowshoe Hare	■
Black Bear	☐	Moose	◪	Squirrels	■
Coyote	◪	Porcupine	■	Striped Skunk	■
Harbor Seal	■	Raccoon	■	White-Tailed Deer	■
Little Brown Bat	■	Red Fox	■		
Long-Tailed Weasel	◪	River Otter	◪		

BIRDS

American Black Duck	■	Double-Crested Cormorant	■	Osprey	■
Bald Eagle	■	Downy Woodpecker	■	Peregrine Falcon	◪
Barred Owl	■	Great Black-Backed Gull	■	Pileated Woodpecker	■
Black-Backed Woodpecker	◪	Great Blue Heron	■	Purple Sandpiper	◪
Black Guillemot	■	Great Horned Owl	■	Ring-Billed Gull	■
Broad-Winged Hawk	■	Guillemot	■	Ruffed Grouse	■
Bufflehead	■	Hairy Woodpecker	■	Saw-Whet Owl	■
Common Eider	■	Herring Gull	■	Snowy Owl	◪
Common Loon	■	Kestrel	■	Spotted Sandpiper	■
Common Merganser	■	Laughing Gull	■	Spruce Grouse	■
Common Raven	■	Leach's Storm-Petrel	■	Turkey Vulture	■
Common Tern	■	Mallard	■	Warblers	■
				Woodcock	■
				Wood Duck	◪

Always remember there are no guarantees in wildlife watching—but that is what makes each sighting an adventure!

Successful wildlife encounters require knowledge of the animal's habits and habitats, when and where to look for them, and a great deal of patience. Remember: Avoid any behavior on your part that would bring stress to wildlife, and don't get too close.

MAMMALS

BEAVER

Of all the park mammals the beaver (*Castor canadensis*) is the easiest to find for it is never far from its pond; about 300 feet is its limit when tree cutting. Beavers are the largest rodents in North America. They are covered with a luxurious coat of brown fur and individuals weigh anywhere from 27 to 67 pounds. Males and females are about equal in size ranging in length from 32 to 48 inches long. The animal's unique paddle-like tail alone is from 12 to 20 inches.

Beavers are excellent swimmers but are clumsy on land; their torpedo-shaped body, webbed feet, and unusual tail are designed for living in the water. If you see one, it will most likely be swimming along in its pond with just its head showing above the surface. In the water, the beaver's large flat tail generally acts as a rudder but it is very muscular and can also be used for a burst of speed in the water. When startled by humans a beaver slaps its flat tail on the surface sending water spraying out in all directions, then it dives out of sight. On land, the animal uses its tail as a prop for sitting upright as it chews on a tree.

Beavers are active throughout the year although inclement weather may keep them in their lodges. They especially avoid hard rain. Actually, the best time for observation is in the evening, for beavers are active mostly at night. To see them, a great deal of patience is needed, and insect protection is recommended.

Beavers mate for life. Young beavers usually stay with their parents for two years before starting out on their own, so the beaver colony often numbers up to a dozen members including the parents, the new kits and the yearlings.

The beaver lodge is most often out in the water well away from shore but some beavers build bank dens. Those in the park tend to have lodges surrounded by water because the banks are pretty rocky. Even if you do not see the actual beaver, its dam is impressive and conspicuous. It provides the beaver the depth of water needed to float food and building material to its lodge. The water also furnishes protection as a place in which to disappear and escape predators. A large dam is probably the work of several generations of beavers. A beaver pond provides an excellent wildlife habitat for many other creatures too, such as fish, frogs, turtles, salamanders, insects, ducks, and herons.

Where To Find Beavers

On the eastern side of the island in the park you will have easy access to several beaver ponds. You can park at the Bear Brook Picnic Area on the Park Loop Road.

A short walk from the Eagle Lake Parking area on Route 233 also gives you nice views of several beaver ponds. Walk out on the carriage road toward Witch Hole Pond and Breakneck Pond.

At the Visitor Center on Route 3 you can check the park list of daily field trips and sign up for the Beaver Walk.

RIVER OTTER

River otters (*Lutra canadensis*) are secretive creatures and it is difficult to predict where to find them, but occasionally they can be viewed as they swim in local ponds and in the saltwater along the shore in their search for fish, frogs, salamanders, earthworms, small snakes and even some plants. The sleek, brown body is muscular and the short legs are powerful. Some otters are residents on outer islands. (We do not have sea otters on the East Coast, so any otter seen in the park is a river otter.)

If you do not get to see otters, you may still find their slides in either mud or snow. They slide on their bellies with feet folded back out of the way down a steep muddy bank into the water. The same action is enjoyed in the winter on snow and ice. Since otters are large mammals, from 3 to 4 feet long not including the tail and weighing up to 30 pounds, look for a wide packed-down area on a steep bank leading into the water. Although it is nice to think their mud or snow slides are just for fun, otters do also use them for moving about more easily, especially in the snow. The otter's

hind foot has five fully webbed toes with claws at the tip and is about 4.3 to 5.9 inches long—big compared to the foot of its weasel cousins!

The big fire on MDI in 1947 that burned thousands of acres had a great influence on the otter population. The mature forests of spruce and fir were replaced by much more diverse woods that included aspen, birch and other deciduous species as well as conifers. With more food to their liking beaver numbers increased, which in turn increased the number of ponds providing stable water levels year-round. Those ponds provided a good supply of year-round food for otters in the form of fish and amphibians. Otters may use abandoned beaver lodges for denning and resting sites. Or they may enlarge a muskrat house or woodchuck burrow for their den.

Where To Find River Otters

With the increased number of visitors to Mount Desert Island and especially the park, local otters retire to whatever inaccessible wetlands are available, even on offshore islands.

HARBOR SEAL

Seals can be seen from the shore as they swim along and occasionally bask on a rock in the sun, but the best views come from a boat. They seem to be curious about the activities of humans and will often come close to boats during their foraging hours at high tide. So take a naturalist cruise, if you want to see seals.

The common harbor seal (*Phoca vitulina*) is about 5 feet long. Its color varies, so you will see reddish, brown, black, gray and white harbor seals.

Watch carefully when you are looking at seals for you may also see the larger (up to 8 feet) gray seal (*Halichoerus grypus*) along with the harbor seals. The gray seal's head is reminiscent of that of a horse and thus earns this mammal its nickname "horsehead."

It is not uncommon to find harbor seals resting on a mudflat close to shore or relaxing on the exposed ledges at half tide. The seal's habits are closely connected to the changing tides. They rest in groups at the early falling tide and then disperse and hunt for food during the high tide.

In spring the pregnant females and pups stay on protected ledges; the males and juveniles stay apart at this time. Only when the pups are weaned do the herds reassemble. Sunning themselves on exposed rocky ledges is a common activity, although less frequent in the winter months.

Seal pups stay on shore without the mother, so never pick them up or disturb them. If you think a young seal has a problem, notify a park ranger.

The harbor seal is well distributed along the Maine coast. It is also found on both sides of the North Atlantic and Pacific Oceans and it is a permanent resident in the Gulf of Maine.

Where To Find Harbor Seals

Sit on the rocks at the Seawall Picnic Area on 102 A and watch the water—seals often swim by.

Seals are also seen in the Pretty Marsh area of the park on the western side of the island off 102.

They can be seen from shore at the Blagden Nature Preserve at Indian Point, which is reached from the Indian Point Road in Town Hill. When visiting this preserve be respectful of the adjacent private property.

RED FOX

In Acadia National Park you will now find two wild representatives of the dog family: the red fox and the coyote. The red fox (*Vulpes vulpes*) is quite commonly seen. This canid resembles a small collie except for its color. Males tend to be bigger than females, weighing from 8 to 12 pounds.

The red fox ranges from 35 to 41 inches in total length, has a long and pointed muzzle and large, pointed and erect ears. Sporting a bushy tail, from 12 to 15 inches long, and wearing a coat of dense, long, silky fur in red, brown, gray-brown or black, it is a strikingly beautiful animal. There are three distinct color phases and although color varies with individuals the tip of the tail is always white.

At night you may see these timid mammals along the roadsides. During the day, especially early in the morning or on a foggy Maine day, you might also spy one hunting in a meadow.

Even in sub-zero weather this fox sleeps outside. Its den is mainly used for the pups. Except for denning, these mammals are solitary creatures.

Island residents frequently feed a neighborhood fox, but although it is fun for the humans it is not healthy for the fox. The fox becomes too tame and trusting and this often results in the animal's death when it meets an unfriendly human or encounters a fierce dog. Enjoy watching foxes but do not feed them.

Where To Find Red Foxes

Look for foxes along any park and island road after dark. Go out early in the morning and look for them in meadows or fields. Early morning golfers often see them on local courses. Watch for foxes any time you hike the carriage roads.

The salt marsh near the Trenton Bridge coming onto MDI is also a good place to look for foxes. Especially look in the Thunderhole area on the Park Loop Road.

COYOTE

The coyote (*Canis latrans*) looks a bit like a small collie but is more slender with pointed ears and a drooping bushy tail. Its muzzle is long and narrow. The fur of the coyote is coarse, long and dense. Although both sexes tend to look alike, showing only slight seasonal color variations, color does vary with individuals. Buff, gray, brown and black seem to be the dominant colors. This animal's annual molt starts in June and is not completed until the fall of the year. They wear their prime coats from November through February. It has been noted that coyotes in the eastern states tend to be more robust than those in the west.

Coyotes originally ranged only in the western half of North America, but as its habitat changed and wolves disappeared, coyotes began moving east. They first appeared in Maine in the 1940s but it was not until the mid 1980s that the first documented sighting of a coyote was reported on Mount Desert Island. They continued to be seen in more regular numbers and in the 1990s many island residents are able to enjoy listening to the coyote chorus on moonlit nights.

The presence of coyotes is welcomed by some, feared and misunderstood by others. The coyote is no real threat to the deer population and is actually a help in natural population control. There are no other large predators on Mount Desert Island, and since hunting is not allowed in the park they play an important role in keeping the deer herd in balance. Coyotes are opportunists in the choice of food and will eat a wide variety of dead and living animals as well as blueberries and insects. They avoid humans very well.

Where To Find Coyotes

Driving slowly through the park and around the island at night is the best way to glimpse a coyote. A coyote's yellow eyes in the headlights are often the first thing visitors notice.

29

Although coyotes are chiefly nocturnal you may also see them during the day at times. Hikers moving quietly along the carriage roads can come upon them quite unexpectedly. Also if you are observant you may find their scat (droppings) on the ground, often in the middle of the trail.

If you are camping in one of the woodland campgrounds, listen for their yapping at night. They often seem to howl for pleasure or to call a warning to other coyotes. It can be quite a musical sound, full of howls, warbles and other yippings. You will note that the sounds often start and stop as if turned on and off by a switch. Domestic dogs sometimes join in the chorus from the safety of their owners' living room!

WHITE-TAILED DEER

White-tailed deer (*Odocoileus virginianus borealis*) are plentiful and widely distributed in the park. You will probably get your first view of this beautiful mammal as it grazes alongside the road. White-tailed deer are from 3 to 3 1/2 feet high at the shoulder and weigh anywhere from 50 to about 250 pounds. They seem always ready to bound off, for their long thin legs give them the ability to run quickly and jump easily. In the summer their coat is reddish tan; in winter it is more gray. The conspicuous white tail, giving the deer its name, is often raised when the animal is startled and fleeing. It is the animal's signaling "flag."

Male deer have moderately spreading large antlers which can be formidable weapons when the bucks fight during the breeding season. The antlers are shed annually from mid-December to mid-January. In April or May they start to grow again so they will reach their prime in September in time for a new breeding season. Older deer tend to have large antlers but the quality and availability of food plus heredity also affects antler growth.

Deer are protected on the island but their numbers do become reduced by coyotes hunting them. Coyotes are their natural predator. If there were no checks and balances on the deer population their numbers would increase and put a strain on the available food supply, and many would starve to death.

Although the early morning hours and evening hours seem to be the best times to see them, deer can be encountered at any hour of the day or night. Driving the roads after dark can be hazardous if you are not aware that they are about. Where there is one deer you will most likely find several more. Honking the horn does not have much affect on them. Flicking your headlights and reducing your speed are the best defensive courses of action. Pay attention to those "deer crossing" road signs!

Where To Find White-Tailed Deer

Look for deer in the early evening near the Wild Flower Gardens of Acadia.

Deer are frequently seen in the big field across from the Ranger's Station at Seawall on 102 A at dusk and early morning.

Look for deer alongside the road on 102 coming into South West Harbor from Echo Lake in the evening and at night.

You may see also them in the daylight along the Park Loop Road and the footpath that starts just above Sand Beach.

MOOSE

Moose (*Alces alces*) are not common in the park, but you may be fortunate enough to meet one in the woods or see one step out onto the road as you drive about the island.

A full grown moose, weighing 1,400 pounds, is about 9 feet long from its big nose to its very short tail and may be as high as 7 1/2 feet at the shoulders. It also has a short neck, high hump on the shoulders, a small rump and long legs. A bull moose can move with grace and speed through the forest and swamps even with a large rack of antlers on his head. Moose antlers are massive. They start growing in April and by August or September are fully developed. The moose usually sheds its antlers in December or January, but may shed as late as March.

Moose are quite nearsighted but they have a keen sense of hearing and smell. If you should see one, do not try to get close! Respect this animal's size and ease of movement in the woods. They usually move off at the sound of a human voice, for man is their chief predator.

Since the lakes in Acadia were formed by glaciers and are too deep to allow moose to feed on submerged vegetation—and local ponds are too heavily populated with people—moose tend to be seen in swamps and woodland areas. Moose go into the water not only to eat but also to avoid biting insects.

As moose browse in winter they seek out conifers and hardwood trees. In spring, summer and early fall they feed on semi-aquatic and aquatic plants such as pondweeds, pickerelweed and other local water plants. At all seasons they prefer twigs and leaves of willows, gray and white birches, mountain alder, maples and viburnums. They must consume large quantities of food since what food they do eat contains such low nutritional value.

Never approach a moose too closely, never try to feed one, and never get between a calf and a mother. As with all wild animals the mother moose defends her young vigorously. Moose can be dangerous. Respect their right to privacy and give them space.

Where To Find Moose

Look for moose tracks and droppings along the trails in the Western Mountain Road area and on the Seal Cove Road near Southwest Harbor. This (mostly dirt) road goes through a portion of the park.

They have been known to step out onto Route 102 between Southwest Harbor and Bass Harbor. Always remember to drive slowly where moose may be present. Be prepared to stop quickly.

BLACK BEAR

A few black bears (*Ursus americanus*) are found in Acadia National Park but they are not often seen on MDI. They are most commonly seen in the area just outside the Schoodic section of the park on the mainland. They are quite common in other areas of the state of Maine.

Although solitary wanderers, and for the most part peaceful, bears are easily provoked and can be dangerous. Never approach them and never try to feed them. If you are camping where bears live, keep a clean camp-site and store food out of their reach—in your car or hung high in a sack in a tree. Bears are often attracted by food smells, so don't keep food in your tent or sleep in your cooking clothes!

Black bears are particularly fond of blueberries, and exciting stories have been told by berry pickers having unexpected encounters with bears in a blueberry patch. When bears are present you are more likely to see signs of them in the woods rather than the animals themselves. They like to rip open rotten tree stumps for ants and their eggs. And the bears' liking for sweets has them raiding bee hives.

Although bears go into a deep sleep in the winter, it is not true hiber-nation, for their heart beat, body temperature and breathing are only slightly reduced. In mid-winter the female gives birth and nurses her very tiny cubs, which weigh only a few ounces at birth. Their eyes do not open for about four weeks. A mother bear is very protective of her cubs.

Where To Find Black Bear

If you should be fortunate enough to see a bear, enjoy the encounter from a good distance!

PORCUPINE

Porcupines (*Erethizon dorsatum*) are nature's living "pin cushions" and the second largest North American rodent (after the beaver). An adult porcupine may weigh from 5 to 25 pounds.

The quills, as many as 30,000, are most dense on the animal's back and the upper surface of the tail. The bases of the quills are yellowish white and the tips are brown or black. At birth the quills are very soft, but after about an hour they harden and become the animal's main defense. Contrary to folklore, quills cannot be thrown, but they do come out of the porcupine's skin easily, especially when an aggravated porcupine slaps its tail. Many a dog owner has had to deal with this when the family pet has aggravated a porcupine and gotten a face full of quills.

Although porcupines are nocturnal creatures you sometimes meet one on a trail or see one in a tree in the daylight hours. Porcupines are large, robust rodents usually seen moving slowly and deliberately on land and in trees. They are not fond of water but they can swim; they can climb easily and most of their time is spent in trees.

Around a camp they sometimes get into trouble because of their liking for salt. In the summer and late winter, especially, they have a craving for salt. Human perspiration, a salt solution, remaining on any axe handle, oar, paddle, or boot that has been touched by humans may be attacked. They will also chew on deer antlers found in the woods for the sodium content.

Where To Find Porcupines

If you drive about in the early evening and scan the young trees along the road, especially the Eagle Lake Road, Route 233, from Somesville to Bar Harbor, you may see their fat, brown bodies sitting on a limb enjoying an evening meal or just sleeping.

Porcupines are slow moving mammals and often seen along the park roads at night. Unfortunately many are killed by motorists, so please drive slowly in the park.

Look for them in apple trees in the fall; they love apples.

RACCOON

Raccoons (*Procyon lotor*) are nocturnal prowlers you will have a good chance of seeing in the park, especially if you are camping. These 20 to 40 pound animals are robust and seem to have a black mask across dark eyes and cheeks. The tail is round, bushy and ringed. Their legs are long and slender. Both male and female look alike.

Never try to feed them. Their cute looks may fool you into thinking they are gentle animals but it is not always so. Watch them from a distance.

Since raccoons are opportunists, they eat just about anything they can find, be it plant or animal food. It is often recounted that raccoons always wash their food before they eat, but this is not so. Actually, away from water raccoons eat food as it is wherever they find it. Raccoons have well developed senses of hearing, sight and touch as well as a good memory.

Where To Find Raccoons

At night, especially around picnic areas or in campgrounds. Since raccoons can climb well, you may see them in a tree looking down at you around your campsite. A nice sight after dark is seeing pairs and family groups of raccoons together crossing the road in an ambling line.

Watch for them alongside the road as you drive around after dark throughout the park.

STRIPED SKUNK

The striped skunk (*Mephitis mephitis*) is a small black and white mammal usually seen ambling along on its short legs searching for insects. The white stripe varies in width, but it stretches from head to tail. These skunks are about the size of a house cat. Because their back legs are longer than their front legs they often look as if they are "jacked up" in the rear. This position is probably most helpful in the animal's search for food as it moves along with nose down using its keen sense of smell.

If a skunk has been disturbed you know they are in the area by that strong, pungent musk odor. When frightened or annoyed this fur bearer can forcibly expel up to a distance of fifteen feet or more, a yellowish, oily fluid from a pair of oval anal glands. Also, as a skunk is killed on the road it involuntarily sprays. Spraying this fluid is the skunk's only means of defense, for the skunk is near sighted, not a fast runner and not a fighter.

Where To Find Striped Skunks

The best place and time to see skunks is in the wee hours of the morning on the streets of any of the towns on the island. After humans have gone to bed and the town is relatively quiet, skunks come out looking for food. They are often seen crossing the street or scooting down a sidewalk and across someone's lawn.

If you camp in the park you may have them rummaging about your campsite after dark. Treat them with respect, talk softly, move slowly and keep your dog quiet and under control. A family of skunks parading along with tails held high is a memorable sight.

MINK

The patient, early morning fisherman may get a glimpse of a mink (*Mustela vison*) making its way along the shore of a pond, lake or brook. Mink are sometimes bold enough to steal a freshly caught fish!

Although about the size of a large ferret, a mink is more robustly built and its fur coat is a dense, thick, soft, dark glossy brown. The toes of its hind feet are slightly webbed to help it move in the water. Mink can dive and swim underwater up to 100 feet.

Mink are wanderers and occupy diverse habitats but are seldom seen far from water. They tirelessly wander a wide range searching for their prey of fish, frogs, turtles, snakes, mice and other food. Their sense of smell is very highly developed and they are skillful hunters.

They may dig their own burrow, use some other animal's burrow, or den under a rock or log from 1 to 3 feet below ground. For safety this den will have several entrances. An old muskrat house is quite acceptable as a den for mink. Kits (baby mink) are born in April or May and at birth are long and skinny, about the size of a cigarette, with fine hairs scarcely covering their pink flesh. In about five weeks their eyes open. The family stays together well into the summer.

Where To Find Mink

They are elusive and not easily found but visitors have seen them around ponds or streams and some marshes at dawn or dusk. Sit quietly, wait, and watch.

It is interesting to note that mink can also be found on the nearby outer islands, as these mammals make use of both fresh– and saltwater food opportunities. The sea mink found along the coast of New England until about 1860 is now extinct.

LONG-TAILED WEASEL

When wildlife watching, keep alert for a skinny little predator, the long-tailed weasel (*Mustela frenata*). These small mammals are found from sea level to timberline, but sitting quietly on a rocky shore is the best place to get a chance to see one. Much larger than a female, an adult male measures from 11.8 to 17.3 inches long including a tail which is from 3.2 to 6.3 inches long. They can weigh around 9 ounces.

They are curious mammals and will come out to take a quick peek at you as they move about in the rocks searching for food. This weasel eats about a third of its weight every twenty-four hours; young growing weasels eat even more. In a single night the long-tailed weasel will perhaps cover seven miles or more in search of mice, birds and their eggs, bats, hares, frogs, earthworms, other prey and even carrion. Although basically nocturnal they are sometimes seen in daylight hours.

As cold weather approaches in mid-October the weasel sheds its brown coat for a white one so the animal can move about in the snowy landscape unseen by predators. The change from white back to brown starts in mid-February and is usually completed by mid-April. The long-tailed weasel has a wide distribution for it can be found from southern Canada to Peru.

Where To Find Long-Tailed Weasels
Your best chance at seeing one is to sit quietly for awhile on the rocks along the Seawall on 102 A or some other rocky shoreline.

LITTLE BROWN BAT
Several species of bats can be seen in the park but the most common is the little brown bat (*Myotis lucifugus*). It is small enough to fit in your hand; total length is from 3.1 to 3.7 inches and the weight is from 0.19 to 0.42 ounces. Although bats are mainly nocturnal these in the north often fly during daylight. On chilly days here in Maine, it is quite normal to see them flying about in the mid-morning sunshine when insects are active.

Bats are a little known natural resource and very valuable because of all the flying insects they consume; one little brown bat can eat 600 mosquitoes in a single hour. Because mosquitoes are part of their diet, bats are very valuable creatures to encourage around your home; many island residents have put up bat houses.

The little brown bat is a master of flight and can fly from 12 to 21 mph. The bone structure of a bat's wing resembles that of a human arm and hand except that bats have very long fingers. Two thin layers of skin stretched between the bat's fingers form its wing so that it can actually fly. Bats are the only mammals able to do so. Other mammals may glide but they do not fly. When moving across tree trunks and the rough surface of a cave or side of a building, bats use their claw-like thumbs to help them. Bats have special tendons in their legs that make it possible for them to hang by their feet when they sleep or roost.

In Maine, bats are a threatened species because of human activities. The areas of big woods with hollow trees in which to live have diminished in the state making available homesites virtually nonexistent. Bats then move into attics, houses, churches and other buildings where they are not always welcomed. Unfortunately bats are often killed in order to remove them from human habitation, instead of relocating them properly and

sealing any places of entry. Bats have also been disturbed by the activities of spelunkers in their roosting caves.

The usually nocturnal habits of bats have made it difficult to appraise
their status on the island and in the park for these interesting mammals
tend to hide during the day. Official records include four species in addi-
tion to the little brown bat in the area: silver-haired bat, small-footed
myotis, hoary bat and red bat.

Where To Find Little Brown Bats

Walk the streets of Bar Harbor in the late evening and look for bats flying about the street lights as they catch insects.

Evening concert goers should watch for them at outdoor concerts as
well as in large churches with the doors left open.

Take a night walk on any of the carriage roads, especially those along
the edge of a small pond.

BIRDS

BALD EAGLE

The adult bald eagle (*Haliaeetus leucocephalus*) is easily recognized with its white head, white tail, dark body and wings, and large size; no other bird looks like it. Young immature eagles appear dark all over; it takes about four years for them to become fully mature adults. During these years the bird's large size helps in identification. Its wingspan is from 6 to 7 1/2 feet.

Maine is the last stronghold of the bald eagle in New England. In Acadia National Park it can be seen near any expanse of fresh- or saltwater where it feeds mostly on dead fish or fish stolen from an osprey. Although the eagle is quite capable of catching its own fish it can be considered a lazy opportunist. An eagle will often wait until an osprey has caught something, then the eagle will intimidate the osprey until it drops the fish and the eagle takes the meal instead. Besides fish, bald eagles also feed on carrion, water

Previous pages' photograph: Flock of Common Terns

46

fowl, squirrels and rabbits. Sometimes it is possible to see eagles, crows and ravens feeding simultaneously at a carcass on the mudflats.

Each year eagles return to the same nest site and make a few renovations. After a good many years the weight of a nest may cause the tree to fall down. Eagles are disturbed by the presence of humans with their noisy traffic and other activities near the nest site. The bird's needs for space and quiet are great, so do respect their privacy and never try to get close to a nest. If you take one of the nature cruises out of Bar Harbor you may be able to see an eagle's nest on one of the Porcupine Islands.

In 1994 the bald eagle in the United States was moved from the endangered species list to the threatened species list. Here on MDI, however, the eagle is still an endangered species, for PCBs and other contaminants are still making the egg shells thin, so many eggs break before hatching. In 1994 seven pairs nested on MDI but only one pair successfully raised young.

Where To Find Bald Eagles

Look for them in the Somesville area near the library and over Somes Pond, and Somes Sound.

Eagles are often seen in the park along the Seawall, Wonderland, and Ship Harbor areas on 102 A, and in Bass Harbor.

Look for them at the Trenton Bridge near the Park Information Center, and along the section of the Park Loop Road called the Ocean Drive.

Take one of the many nature cruises in local waters to get good views of eagles. They are frequently seen from sailing and cruise boats around the island. The mere presence of an eagle along the shore sends nearby gulls into the air—a good clue eagles are in an area.

Watch for them as you hike on any of the island mountains.

PEREGRINE FALCON

The peregrine falcon (*Falco peregrinus*) is the world's fastest bird and can dive through the air at incredible speed. It has been clocked accurately at over 100 mph as it plunged downward through the air. In regular flight, it flies at about 60 mph.

The peregrine is about the size of a crow and is readily recognized as a falcon by its long pointed wings and long narrow tail. The back is slate gray, the breast light colored and the head very dramatic looking with its black sideburns.

The peregrine falcon was first sighted on MDI in 1936 but during the late 1950s the peregrine became a non-breeding bird in Acadia National Park on Mount Desert Island, a direct result of the use of pesticides. Nest robbing, trapping, and shooting first contributed to their downfall but the later use of pesticides completed the job. It also is quite probable that there were never more than two pairs of these falcons on the island.

One aerie, or nesting site, was located on the steep slope of Champlain Mountain near Bar Harbor and the other on the Eagle Cliffs of St. Sauveur bordering Somes Sound. A new chick hatching program has this species once again nesting on the cliffs of Champlain Mountain near the Precipice Trail. In order to protect the birds this trail is closed until the nesting season is over and the fledglings have left the nest in mid-summer. This reintroduction program started in 1984 and has been very successful.

Although peregrines usually nest on precipitous cliffs they will also nest under suspension bridges and atop tall city buildings. When the young falcons begin to grow they may be seen sitting at the edge of their nest on the cliff and perhaps flapping their wings to build flying strength. At this time they look white and fluffy. Once they leave the nest to fly they can be seen practicing flying above the cliff or perched in a tree in the vicinity.

From March to mid-April it is possible to see the courtship activities of this special bird. Adult falcons fly close to each other near the nesting cliff performing in-flight acrobatics and even feeding each other. They are very vocal at this time. From mid-April through May while the birds are nesting you may also get a chance to see the adult birds exchange food in mid-air.

Where To Find Peregrine Falcons

The best place to look is in the vicinity of the Precipice Trail on the Park Loop Road. During the nesting season a park volunteer is on duty at the Precipice parking lot from 9 a.m. to noon to answer questions about the falcons. They also give visitors an opportunity to see them at and around the aerie through a spotting scope.

Look for peregrines as you hike the upper levels of any of the mountains. During fall migration check the Beech Mountain Fire Tower Area, which is reached off Route 102 just outside of Southwest Harbor, and also the upper slopes of Cadillac Mountain. You can drive to the top of Cadillac Mountain.

OSPREY

The osprey—or fish hawk—is a familiar sight over any body of water in the park or on MDI. The osprey (*Pandion haliaetus*) has a wingspan of up to 6 feet, a dark back and a white belly. Although the head is largely white it has a broad black patch through the cheeks. It can be differentiated from an eagle merely by the way it flies, for ospreys have a noticeable crook at the "elbow" of the wing. They also flap a lot and then hover in one spot before diving. Eagles soar more, flap less and hold their wings flat.

The nest of the osprey is an impressive collection of branches, sticks, driftwood, seaweed and the like. Year after year ospreys will return to the same nest only adding a few more sticks and such to the structure until the nest may weigh several hundred pounds. Nest sites in the park vary; they may be high in the trees (possibly 60 feet up) or on a rock along the seashore. The adults make quite a fuss if you come close to their nest; they sound a plaintive, shrill, quickly repeated whistle and fly about overhead. Retreat at such a time so the birds will not be agitated.

When the baby ospreys are first hatched the adult male brings fish back to the nest, and tears it into bite size morsels which he gives to the female to chew. She then feeds the young. Later whole fish are dropped into the nest and the nestlings feed themselves. The young are in the nest for about two months. During this time the hot summer temperatures may make the young uncomfortable so the mother osprey spreads her wings and stands overhead to give them shade. After leaving the nest, young osprey learn to fish on their own.

These large raptors search for fish in both fresh– and saltwater, hovering in the air for several seconds before plunging onto their prey. When you see an osprey make a successful dive you will notice that it prefers to carry the fish with its head forward. If the fish happens to be caught in the opposite position the bird will turn it around in mid-air. Watch also for the habit of washing its feet after a fishy meal. The osprey will glide low and let its feet drag in the water in order to wash off any fish slime still on the talons.

As with many birds, but especially the eagle, osprey and peregrine falcon, DDT, PCBs and other chlorinated hydrocarbons almost eliminated the species. Then in 1972 DDT use was banned in this country and the osprey slowly recovered from its decline. Maine now has the largest population in New England, though it remains a threatened species.

Where To Find Ospreys

A good place to see them is near the small pond next to the library in Somesville on 102. Or take a natural history cruise; you will likely be shown a nest on the rocks close to one of the nearby islands.

Visit the Nature Conservancy's Blagden Nature Preserve on Indian Point Road, not far from the Town Hill Country Store. There is an osprey nest on the property. Check with the naturalist on duty for information.

BROAD-WINGED HAWK

If a small chunky hawk, about the size of a crow, rises up from the side of the road with a snake dangling from its claws, you most likely have seen a broad-winged hawk (*Buteo platypterus*) in action.

This common buteo has a heavy body and short wide tail. Look also for the manner of banding on the tail, for the white bands are about as wide as the black.

This hawk is very fond of snakes as well as insects, small birds, frogs, rodents, fish and even earthworms. With such a wide variety of food on its menu the bird has plenty to eat.

Of all the hawks, the broad-winged hawk in the Maine woods is quite tame and will sit still or only move a short distance when approached.

During the fall migration many hawk watchers gather on Beech Mountain. Because MDI is on a flightline it is well worth visiting the park in September to see this natural event. The birds use the warm thermals created by the mountains on the island and will sometimes be seen at very close range as they pass. At other times watchers will see hundreds of birds in a whirling "kettle" high in the sky moving south.

With patience hawk watchers on Beech Mountain will see some

birds passing by very closely and feeding only a few yards away. Take your binoculars and a lunch and spend some hours on a mountain top in September to see the migration.

In the winter an occasional migrating rough-legged hawk (*Buteo lagopus*) will be seen in coastal marshes. Time of the year and its habit of hovering make it easy to identify.

Where To Find Broad-Winged Hawks

Beech Mountain on the western side of the island off 102. Follow signs to the fire tower and hike up the rest of the mountain.

Drive to the top of Cadillac Mountain in Bar Harbor and sit on the rocks and watch the sky.

Look for broad-winged hawks in the woods, sitting in a tree at the edge of the woods or as they fly up from the side of the road.

The Bass Harbor Marsh is an especially good place to look for rough-legged hawks.

COMMON LOON

The distinctive, yodeling call of the loon is a true wilderness sound and can be heard in numerous places in the park. Loons (*Gavia immer*) are not difficult to identify in the water, sometimes riding high, and sometimes low with only their head and the top of their back showing. The bird's head and neck are glossy black with a white collar; the back is "checkered" black and white. Occasionally you will see them on their sides in the water with their white bellies exposed. Some visitors confuse the loon with the cormorant but if you remember that the loon's head is held so that the bill is horizontal with the water and the bill of the cormorant is held tipped slightly skyward you will be able to tell them apart. Also the cormorant is all black.

Loons look quite different in the winter. They are then mostly dark gray on the top of the head, back and neck contrasted with white cheeks, throat and underparts.

There are several large ponds and lakes within the park where loons may nest. They build their nests right at water level—they're ill equipped for walking, with their legs placed so far back on their body. Unfortunately, the waves from fast moving boats or water skiers may wash right up over the nests and ruin the eggs. Loons prefer quiet, secluded bodies of water—such as those on which canoes and non-motorized craft are used. And unless repeatedly disturbed they return year after year to the same nesting spot.

54

When young loons are hatched the parent carries them about on its back for a few days, after which they remain afloat much of the time until they are grown. Even when just a day or two old young loons are able to swim and dive. Young have been seen early in the morning getting exercise with their parents as they all race across a lake using their broad foot paddles for propulsion and their half-extended wings for support.

Where To Find Loons

Walk around Jordan Pond just off the Park Loop Road and you may see loons. Echo Lake is another good location, especially early in the morning or late in the day when it is quiet.

Long Pond on the western side of MDI is a good place to look; however, the trail is a little rough.

Loons winter on the ocean and in local bays and harbors but as soon as the freshwater ponds and lakes are free of ice they move back to them.

DOUBLE-CRESTED CORMORANT

Cormorants (*Phalacrocorax auritus*) are dark water birds with snake-like necks, appearing like feathered submarines. To distinguish them from the commonly seen loons also on the water, look for the cormorant's bill pointed slightly upward (the loon holds its bill level). In the summer two curly black crests can be seen on the cormorant's head but in the winter there are no crests. These cormorants begin arriving at the end of March and until their long migrating lines and Vs leave in the fall they are a familiar bird along the shore and on the lakes. When they take off they look a bit clumsy until airborne with necks outstretched.

Cormorants nest on offshore islands near the park and you can easily see their nesting colonies if you take one of the local nature cruises. Some nests are in the trees, others are on the ground made of sticks and seaweed. A nesting colony is a noisy, smelly place with calling babies, nests placed closely together, and many well worn paths into the area made by cormorant feet padding along to and fro.

The adults flying about in the colony usually land near the edge and walk to their particular nesting spot so the nesting colony becomes a maze of these little paths.

Cormorants dive for their meals of fish from a sitting position and actually swim underwater in pursuit of fish. Since their plumage is not waterproof they must perch on rocks, posts or buoys later with their wings outstretched to dry in their typical "spread eagle" or "preaching from the mount" position. Locally, they are often nicknamed shags.

Where To Find Double-Crested Cormorants

Visit the local harbors and dock area; any shoreline location may present cormorants.

Hamilton Pond on Route 3 in Salisbury Cove is visible from the road and cormorants are often seen sitting on half sunken logs and tree limbs.

Walk out on the Bar at Bar Harbor. Or take any of the nature cruises and you are likely to see cormorants, swimming, flying and standing about.

HERRING GULL

Herring gulls (*Larus argentatus*) are abundant throughout the park year-round. The body is white with a gray mantle, black wingtips and flesh-colored legs. They have a red spot on their bills. It does, however, take three years for the young gulls to assume this coloring; in the meantime they are dusky brown the first year and mottled brown and white the second. Herring gulls nest on the outer islands such as uninhabited Great Duck Island. Although found mainly on saltwater they do go to ponds and inlets for drinking and bathing.

The herring gull's nest is a cup of grass, seaweed and stems on the ground, on rocks or in thick vegetation. Into this nest two or three eggs are laid. When the downy young hatch, the parents protect them from weath-

er and other enemies. The young herring gull pecks at the red dot on the parent's bill to make it regurgitate food. When the breeding season is over herring gulls scatter along the coast.

Herring gulls are scavengers feeding in local dumps, gathering where fish are being cleaned at sea or in the harbors and devouring the waste tossed away. They also eat dead fish washed up on the beach. Residents on the island often have them coming to their bird feeders if bread is offered.

Gulls have an interesting way of feeding on mussels, sea urchins and other such food with a hard shell. With these items they fly over a hard-surfaced area, preferably flat rocks, and drop the hard encased food. Immediately the bird then drops down to determine whether the shell has broken open and is ready to eat. They may have to repeat this action many times before being able to eat.

The gull's call is a familiar sound in the park and it is very interesting to be able to see the bird bend forward just a bit, open its mouth and make that loud, melodious distinctive gull sound.

Once you have learned to recognize the herring gull you will easily notice the much larger great black-backed gull (*Larus marinus*), with its black back and wings. Black-backed gulls are aggressive and definitely the dominant gull. Its voice is lower and a bit more harsh than that of the herring gull.

On the breeding islands offshore, black-backed gulls are voracious feeders on the eggs and young of other birds, especially sea birds. In the winter black-backs and herring gulls associate freely on seemingly good terms but during the breeding season they are enemies.

Where To Find Herring Gulls

They can be seen anywhere along the coast but especially at the Seawall picnic area, at the Schoodic portion of the park, and along the Park Loop Road. Any of the local harbors and docks are good places to see these gulls.

They also frequent freshwater lakes such as Echo Lake, Long Pond and Jordan Pond for drinking and bathing.

GREAT BLUE HERON

The arrival of spring is often associated with the coming of the first robin but in Acadia the sight of a great blue heron (*Ardea herodias*) standing in the marshes or out on the mudflats signals the end of winter and the start of the new season. These large herons stand about 4 feet tall and have a wingspan as great as that of an eagle, from 42 to 52 inches. Average weight of this heron is only 6 to 8 pounds. Its color is blue-gray with two black crown stripes and a yellow bill. The great white heron found in Florida is a color phase of the great blue heron.

Locally, the great blue heron is often called simply a "crane" but this is in error. It is not a crane. Cranes are long-legged, long-necked birds, superficially like the large great blue heron but cranes are more robust and fly with heads and necks outstretched. The great blue heron flies with its head and neck folded back and with its long legs trailing far behind. This very large heron is often seen on the edges of freshwater ponds, coastal coves and marshes anywhere on the island.

There are nesting colonies on Ironbound Island in Frenchman Bay and on Hardwood Island in Blue Hill Bay. In these small colonies of perhaps 10 to 30 pairs, the stick nests are usually placed in the uppermost branches of a tree. Great blue herons tend to return each year to a successful nesting site enlarging and reusing old nests. Isolation is of prime importance in choosing a nest site.

Many say there is nothing beautiful about a baby heron; they have been described as the ugliest birds in the world. When the parent birds are away the young tend to stay crouched down and out of sight but with the return of the parents a great squawking and moving about begins as the young ones anticipate being fed. Their food at this time is predigested or partially digested fish which is pumped into the young bill. This transfer is accomplished as the young one grabs the parent's beak crosswise in its own.

As you wander about in the park along the coast, or by any freshwater pond where this big heron might be able to catch a meal you will have ample opportunities to observe the bird in action. It stands motionless, like

a picturesque giant, waiting for an unsuspecting frog or fish to come within range of its spear-like bill which can move at lightening speed. Rarely does the bird miss its prey. It is very special to see one of these herons feeding at twilight silhouetted in the waning light.

Where To Find Great Blue Herons

With your binoculars, scan the mudflats on Thompson Island across from the information center after you cross the bridge onto MDI.

Another excellent place to see herons is at the Bass Harbor Marsh bridge on 102 between Southwest Harbor and Bass Harbor, or walk out on the bar at Bar Island in Bar Harbor.

Also, using your car as a blind you can watch the bird without disturbing it. A nice place to do this is along the one way road in the Schoodic portion of the park.

COMMON TERN

The little "mackerel gull," as this bird is called by local fishermen is a beautiful part of the scene in Acadia. Terns (*Sterna hirundo*) look like dainty, elegant, small gulls over the water. They have black caps, swallow-like forked tails, orange-red feet and on the breeding bird the bill is orange red with a black tip.

These attractive terns fly listlessly along over the water and beaches until they discover a small school of fish and then the action begins. Terns hover for a moment then plunge headlong down into the water for the small fish. It is a noisy feeding time when terns find large schools of fish in the harbor. The call is a harsh rolling "*tee ar-r-r-r*," almost musical but with a bit of wildness. Sometimes when very agitated they emit a rapidly repeated and vibratory "*tu tut*," or "*kik, kik, kik*," followed by a piercing, screaming tear. The rapidly repeated notes and the rattling scream sound almost angry.

Feeding terns can be helpful to the fishermen, for their activity often indicates the presence of bluefish. The small fish on which the bluefish feed are driven to the surface in dense schools to escape the bigger fish below. The terns see the small fish and start to feed on them. As soon as one tern discovers the good feeding opportunity others quickly arrive and it is an exciting scene with rushing fish, and the air full of terns plunging, diving and screaming. Terns plunge into the water like winged arrows, and just as they enter the water they fold their wings.

Common terns hardly build a nest at all, they merely excavate a slight hollow in the sand or pebbly beach. Both parents take regular turns sitting on the eggs. The newly hatched baby stays in its nest for one or two days then leaves and wanders aimlessly about in the vicinity of the nest. It seems from various studies done in the colonies that identification of

offspring by the parents is by sight and, especially, smell. From birth the young terns are fed by the parents until they are fully grown, well able to fly, and have been taught to fish for themselves.

There are no nesting terns in the park but bird restoration projects are under way on specially chosen islands nearby and on Petit Manan Wildlife Refuge. These projects are being carried out by the United States Fish and Wildlife Service, The College of the Atlantic, The National Audubon Society and other private groups. Restoration efforts started in 1985.

In the fall, terns desert their breeding grounds and wander about in loose scattered flocks. At such times they will gather on sand bars standing about facing the wind and sleeping.

Where To Find Common Terns

Look for terns in local harbors and from along the Park Loop Road, or on the Bar leading to Bar Island in Bar Harbor.

WOODCOCK

The first call of the woodcock (*Scolopax minor*) when it returns in the spring brings island birders out in the evening to watch this comical shorebird in its nighttime courting ritual, known as the woodcock's sky dance. The woodcock is a short and squat brown bird with its feathers in a dead leaf pattern. It looks almost neckless and the bird's big head, bulging eyes and very long bill make it quite easy to recognize. Added to the woodcock's interesting appearance is its startling courtship performance.

The male woodcock struts around on the ground in an open field or at the edge of a clearing, making a nasal "*bzzzzzping*" sound. Each time the sound is made the bird bends forward a bit, then at the proper moment leaves the ground and flies high into the air. At the pinnacle of his flight the bird sings a very musical song before plummeting back to earth and landing almost exactly at the spot from where it took off. The whole procedure is repeated for hours. To see the bird performing this ritual you must listen for its nasal peep then gradually sneak up on the bird each time it launches itself into the air. With patience you will be able to get quite close; in the beam of a flashlight you can see the "dance."

The woodcock's bill is truly an amazing tool and is well adapted in reaching its food down in the mud. The bill is from 2 to 3 inches long and hinged about half way down. While feeding, woodcocks probe deep into muddy spots for worms. They push their long bills down into the soft ooze right up to their high-set eyes. With the bill buried in the mud the bird is able to hinge it open and seize the worm or other edible creature. If the food morsel is not too large the bird does not have to pull its bill out of the mud in order to eat it—it seems to be sucking the food out of the mud. This is probably how it got its nickname "bog sucker." This feeding habit makes woodcocks very vulnerable to ground predators and in many areas their numbers have decreased considerably. They have also been adversely affected by the destruction of fields and open areas they use as "dancing grounds."

Where to Find Woodcocks

One good evening dancing area is in the field across 102 A in front of the Ranger's house near Seawall.

LEACH'S STORM-PETREL

Petrels are small, dark and swallow-like birds with a rump that is usually white. The Leach's storm-petrel (*Oceanodroma leucorhoa*) has a forked tail and a bounding, butterfly-like flight. It nests in burrows in the ground and during the breeding season pairs of them are very active at night for it is then that the parents exchange nesting duties. While one parent incubates, the other is out at sea. The single baby petrel stays in its burrow for over two months before going to sea with its parents.

You may also see the Wilson's petrel in this area, but it breeds in the southern hemisphere. This small black sea bird has a white rump patch and a tail that is even at the end. It skims over the water like a swallow and habitually follows boats which the Leach's storm-petrel rarely does.

Just a few miles offshore are colonies of Leach's storm-petrels on both Little Duck Island, protected by The National Audubon Society, and Great Duck Island (now a sanctuary), under the protection of the Nature Conservancy. Because of the islands' fragile natures, visitors are welcome only by special permission.

The two islands are visible from Seawall Beach on 102 A. Little Duck Island is on the left and Great Duck Island is on the right.

Most of the petrel's life is spent exclusively on and above the open ocean. The bird only comes to land to nest.

Where To Find Storm-Petrels

You must go out on the open ocean from one of many boat trips available locally to see petrels.

BLACK GUILLEMOT

The picturesque Maine coast would not be the same without this compact, thin-billed bird locally called the "little sea pigeon." For visitors in the summer months it appears dark with very noticeable white wing patches. If you should be watching this bird at close range you might get an opportunity to see its bright red feet and perhaps the red lining of its mouth. In the winter the black guillemot (*Cepphus grylle*) looks quite different, for then the bird is mainly salt and pepper colored, but still retains its white wing patches.

Guillemots fly close to the water with strong, swift and rapid wing strokes, white patches flashing and red feet trailing behind. They also "fly" underwater, using their wings to propel themselves as they swim after their prey. On the coast of Maine they feed largely on rock eels (small fish found at low tide under loose stones).

Observant birders on MDI in the spring watch the amorous antics of the guillemot. The male bird swims furiously after his chosen mate and will even run along on the water in his excitement. If this doesn't work for him he tries hovering momentarily in the air above her with the intention of dropping suddenly on her back. Being a bit clumsy he frequently misses the mark and has to begin all over again.

Guillemots nest along the rocky coast in some suitable crevice under loose rocks or boulders above the high water mark or on a rocky cliff, the more remote the better. The usual two eggs are often laid on a rough bed of pebbles, broken stones or shells. After hatching, the young remain on the ledge or near the nest and are fed by their parents until fully fledged and ready to learn to fly.

No matter what time of the year you visit Acadia National Park you can see guillemots out on the saltwater anywhere along the shore.

Where To Find Guillemots

The Seawall stretch of the park is a good place to see these birds from the beach. Also go to the Bass Harbor Head Lighthouse and scan the waters in front of the lighthouse.

The dock area in Bar Harbor and anywhere along the Park Loop Road are other good locations. Binoculars are helpful in seeing this bird.

COMMON MERGANSER

If you visit Acadia Park in the summer, you will likely see the common merganser (*Mergus merganser*) on a freshwater lake or pond. Hikers along the shores of Long Pond and Jordan Pond often get glimpses of females with their broods of young.

The female common merganser has a crested, rusty-colored head, a red bill and red feet. The male of this species is known by its long white body, black back and green-black head. It has an orange bill and feet, and his breast is tinged with a delicate peach color. In flight the male shows more white on body and wings than any other duck. With its long slender head and neck outstretched you will find it simple to identify.

This merganser shows a great preference for freshwater and will remain inland in the winter wherever it can find open water. Since it is a heavy bodied bird it sometimes experiences great difficulty in rising from the surface, and has to patter along for a considerable distance. When well into flight, however, it is strong and swift. It is an excellent diver and a fast swimmer on the surface so few fish escape. When feeding in flocks there is a good deal of splashing, diving and rushing about. Fishes make up the bulk of their diet and they are voracious feeders.

These ducks prefer to nest in holes in trees and cliffs but when these are absent the bird will choose a ground site. The male deserts the female while she is incubating the eggs; family cares belong entirely to the mother. Young birds hatched in an elevated nest instantly respond to the call of their mother and jump to the ground. They go readily to water. It is a lovely sight to see a mother merganser floating along on the pond with her downy little ones following behind with perhaps one or two babies riding on her back. The young are good swimmers right from the start, and if she dives, they can follow her underwater. The mother merganser will use herself as a decoy if danger seems to warrant it and she will pretend to have a broken wing in order to lure the dog or interested human away from the

young. At such times the young propel themselves at high speed into hiding along the shore. When the danger is passed she rejoins them.

Where To Find Common Mergansers

Bubble Pond is a good place to look and is easily reached from the Park Loop Road on the two-way section. They can also be seen on Jordan Pond on the same road. A walk on the trail around Jordan Pond often gives you glimpses of them, especially along the western side.

COMMON EIDER

Of all the ducks in the park, the common eider (*Somateria mollissima*) is the most commonly seen duck on the saltwater. Males have black and white bodies, black "caps," white cheeks and light green on the back of the head. Females are brown all over. Both sexes have the long sloping bill and chunky, thick-necked look.

These ducks live their lives about shoals along the northern coasts and are seen year-round. Eiders eat mollusks, crustaceans, starfish, sea urchins, plants and fish. They generally nest on the outer islands such as Great Duck, Little Duck, and Petit Manan; a few pairs nest on MDI.

Large rafts (groups floating on the water) of eiders are seen in the early spring as they gather for courtship. The bird's "love note" (sort of an "*aah-ou ah-ee-ou*") frequently repeated is low and pleasing but still can be heard at quite a distance over the water.

Their nests of seaweed, mosses, sticks, leaves and grasses matted together are in a slight depression on the ground. The eider down which is plucked from the mother's breast is so generously supplied in the nest that the eggs can be entirely covered when the mother eider leaves the nest. She alone does the incubating. Sometimes these nests are out in the open, and at other times they are partially or completely hidden under spruce, alder and laurel bushes.

The mothers bring their young on a rather hazardous swim to the shores of MDI to feed and to grow. Their enemies on this journey are many, including seals, gulls, eagles, hawks and fish. However, in spite of the dangers many of them make it, and it is a common sight to see twenty or thirty young with several females moving along together as they feed. Often one male eider accompanies the females and their young, but for the most part the females alone share the care of raising the babies.

Winter visitors to the park also enjoy seeing the little bufflehead (*Bucephala albeola*) swimming in local harbors and along the shores of the island. This small duck is very easy to recognize with its puffy head, marked with a great white patch. The female is darker and is recognized by her white cheek spot. These little tree-hole-nesting ducks breed farther to the north, but can be seen here on the open waters of Echo Lake and along the

Park Loop Road just beyond Sand Beach.

Another commonly seen duck is the the American black duck (*Anas rubripes*). This bird is about the size of a mallard (sometimes it is called a black mallard) and generally dark in color; both sexes look alike (and also quite like female mallards). Its entire plumage is dark mottled brown, which from a distance looks almost black. In the winter they are sometimes confused with scoters which are also black-looking ducks but scoters have stouter heads and shorter necks. In the fall look for black ducks on the waters in the area of the Trenton Bridge, on the water at the Thompson Island picnic area and on the small pond next to the Somesville Library.

Where To Find Common Eiders

Drive along the one-way section of the Ocean Drive for excellent views. You can stop anywhere in the right-hand lane.

Seawall picnic area and the Seawall Causeway on 102 A are good viewing spots. The birds often are quite close to shore.

The Schoodic area of the park also gives excellent views of eiders.

69

PILEATED WOODPECKER

The large flamboyant pileated woodpecker (*Dryocopus pileatus*) with its flaming red crest and loud whooping call is a fairly common sight in Acadia. Until recent years the pileated woodpecker was known only as a bird of wilderness areas but unlike some bird species, this crow-sized woodpecker has adapted to the presence of humans and is now seen all over the island, even along busy highways and in yards and gardens where dead trees can be found. They still need large tracts of woodlands in which to live but they have adapted to second growth forests and younger trees. The bird's loud "*yuk-yuk-yuk-yuk*" call rapidly repeated is exciting to hear and announces the bird's presence in the woods nearby.

If at first you do not see this magnificent woodpecker you will surely see where it has been drilling into the local trees throughout the park. As you hike the trails and carriage roads watch for large rectangular holes made in dead and living trees. This is the work of the pileated. When it drills into the tree it seems to know there are ants and other wood boring insects to be found living inside the tree. With the use of its long, sticky tongue the bird is able to catch and extract ants throughout the partially exposed tunnel system. If the tree is basically healthy the holes will heal in time.

Courtship and territorial activity take place as early as December and January with eggs being laid in April and May. In true woodpecker fashion, courtship and territorial rituals include drumming and "*wukking*" calls. Pileated courtship activity takes place around the roosting and nesting areas with lots of crest raising, wing spreading, head swinging and loud calling.

Nesting holes are quite different from feeding holes. Nesting cavities are excavated by both sexes and will be from 15 to 70 feet above the ground in either a dead limb or trunk in a stand of living trees. The opening is 3 1/2 to 4 1/2 inches in diameter. The excavation may take twenty-five days to complete. After the eggs are laid both parents take turns in the eighteen days required for incubation. These duties are exchanged every two hours during the day and the male occupies the nest at night. Pileateds are devoted parents and family groups remain together until fall.

Where To Find Pileated Woodpeckers

Pileated woodpeckers can be seen throughout the park but sightings are often made and the bird is often heard on the trail around Eagle Lake.

As you walk the carriage roads and trails, watch for their rectangular tree holes. The Little Long Pond area is especially good for seeing these holes easily from the carriage road.

GREAT HORNED OWL

The great horned owl (*Bubo virginianus*) deserves its nickname "Tiger of the Night," for it is a skillful night hunter.

These are large owls; they are as tall as the distance from your elbow to the tips of your fingers, with two ear tufts on the head looking like horns. These tufts are just feathers and have nothing to do with the owl's superb hearing.

The owl's talons are powerful tools for grabbing and holding onto its prey, and the bill is well adapted for tearing its prey into bite-sized morsels. Later, indigestible parts like fur, feathers and bones are regurgitated in pellets under the perch where the owl has eaten its meals. Scientists find them very helpful in learning about the owl's food preferences.

The call of the great horned is like that of a big dog barking in the distance in a pattern of four to seven deep hoots. Young horned owls make sort of a "swishing" sound.

Owls are more often heard than seen no matter where they live. One good way to learn of their whereabouts is to listen for the sound of crows and ravens making a big commotion. This often indicates an owl is trying to rest in a tree and the crows have found it and are teasing the bird. The owl will usually take this annoyance for a certain period of time then fly off to a more secluded spot.

Where To Find Great Horned Owls

The great horned owl has nested in the Ship Harbor area on the west side of the island.

They have also been seen near Eagle Lake.

GALLERY

SNOWSHOE HARE

The snowshoe hare (*Lepus americanus*) is the only type of rabbit found in the park. In summer the fur is brown, but as the season changes to winter it turns white to match the snowy landscape—great for hiding from predators.

It is much bigger than the cottontail and has larger feet. Because its big feet also have hair on the soles, they act like snowshoes to enable the animal to better move about and keep it from sinking in the deep snow.

Snowshoe hares are loners except in the breeding season. Sometimes you will come upon one resting in its "form," which is a special hiding place in the roots of a hollow tree, in a grassy hummock, or next to a hollow log. They seldom dig and they do not go into burrows or holes.

You might see hares crossing the road almost anywhere. Expect them to be erratic in their movement. They often start one way and then turn around quickly and go in the opposite direction. Consequently, many are killed on the highway. Crows, ravens and turkey vultures often feast on these roadkills at the first opportunity.

FLYING SQUIRREL

The red squirrel (*Tamiasciurus hudsonicus*) and gray squirrel (*Sciurus carolinensis*) are found throughout the park. But it is the nocturnal flying squirrel (*Glaucomys volans*) that fascinates many park visitors. They are gentle, social creatures with soft cinnamon-brown fur, big eyes and a broad flattened tail. They are from 9.8 to 11.5 inches long including their 4.5 to 5.3 inch long tail. They weigh from 2 to 4.4 ounces.

Previous pages' photograph: Snowy Owl

Of course, a flying squirrel does not really fly. It travels using its "gliding membrane," a loose fold of skin fully furred on both sides, which extends from the outside of the wrist on the front leg to the ankle of the hind leg. Also using its broad flat tail, the little mammal glides from a high place to a lower place.

Flying squirrels prefer seeds but they also eat bark, leaves, tree buds, lichens, fungi, maple sap, insects and even birds' eggs and fledglings. They in turn are eaten by owls, foxes, weasels, goshawks and domestic cats.

Red and gray squirrels are seen often at park picnic areas, at Blackwoods campground on Route 3, at Seawall on 102 A, at the Bear Brook picnic area on the Park Loop Road and at the Thompson Island picnic area. The best time to get a view of flying squirrels is on a moonlit night along one of the carriage roads where big trees grow. Look for its silhouette as it glides from tree to tree.

SPOTTED SANDPIPER

Many sandpipers migrate through the park but the only one to breed here is the spotted sandpiper (*Actitis macularia*). In breeding plumage this small wading bird's breast is covered with large brown spots.

One easy way to identify this bird is by its habit of bobbing its tail up and down almost continually. If you should flush the bird from one spot it will usually spring into the air while uttering a staccato *"peet! peet!"* then fly on stiff wings close to the water. After making a wide arc it will come back to a location quite close to where it took off.

The spotted sandpiper does not make a very substantial nest and has been known to place it even in a roadside ditch. The downy young instinctively know to take refuge underwater when danger threatens. Adults can even go to the bottom of shallow water and run a short distance.

Watch for these sandpipers along the shores of small ponds and along the seashore. Witch Hole Pond and Breakneck Pond are especially good locations.

Winter and early spring visitors to the park may see the purple sandpiper (*Calidris maritima*), a special visitor from arctic breeding grounds. These stocky shorebirds look dark out on the rocks but in the proper light are quite purple. To see them, go to Seawall, Wonderland and along the rocks at Ship Harbor on the western side of the island in the park off 102 A; and on the sandbar to Bar Island in Bar Harbor.

WOOD DUCK

One of the most beautiful ducks found in the Northeast, and in Acadia in particular, is the wood duck (*Aix sponsa*). The male is highly iridescent, has a white striped, crested head, white throat and glossy purplish chestnut chest that is paler and spotted with white where it meets the white breast. The body, back and rump are a rich bronzy green and the scapulars are black, glossed with purplish green. The bill is red and white and is noticeable from quite a distance.

As the drake sits proudly on the water, he floats high and buoyantly with his tail well elevated. The female has a more subtle beauty showing a white eye ring, white throat and thin crest. Although drab by comparison to the gorgeous male, the female wood duck is more colorful than most female birds. Wood ducks (17 to 20 inches) are smaller than mallards.

This woodland duck is one to look for on the many beaver ponds. Although it is a tree hole nesting duck it will accept a properly built bird house if one is put up in the absence of suitable trees. Such duck boxes are seen throughout the park and on private land. In September these handsome ducks leave the area and head south for the winter. They return once again in April.

Breakneck Pond has good viewing of the wood duck. Also look in the beaver pond on the Park Loop Road in Bar Harbor.

If you'd also like a long walk, another good viewing spot is at Aunt Betty Pond, reached by a carriage road from Route 233.

KESTREL

The smallest relative of the falcon in the park is the colorful kestrel (*Falco sparverius*). It is a common sight sitting on roadside wires or on the top of a post or tree. The bird is not much bigger than a robin and usually sits in an upright position. It has the distinctive habit of hovering over open country; not many birds do this. If you catch a glimpse of it flying along, look for the rust-red tail.

During the summer months, kestrels (or sparrow hawks as they are sometimes called) hunt in open areas for crickets and grasshoppers. As the season advances they take more mice and may also take advantage of small birds at feeders. From their perch on the top of a telephone pole kestrels will intently watch the ground, and when some sort of food comes into sight they swoop down upon it. Whatever food one of these birds has caught is usually taken back to a favorite eating place and ripped apart by the bird's sharp beak.

Look for them in and out of the park wherever the road goes along open fields. Also, look on Route 3 coming into Bar Harbor from the Trenton Bridge.

TURKEY VULTURE

The turkey vulture (*Cathartes aura*) is another very large bird you can see in Acadia Park. Its wingspan is 6 feet. The bird is black, with pale trailing portions on its wings and a featherless head. On adults the head is red; young birds have black heads. Its large size, infrequent flapping of wings and habit of soaring with wings held slightly above the horizontal, make it easy to recognize.

Although most people don't consider this bird particularly beautiful, the featherless head of this carrion eater is perfectly designed for its manner of eating. Long-dead food of any size is prized by the vulture, but it can be very messy. A feathered head stuck into a rotting carcass would be difficult to clean—a naked head eliminates this problem.

For many years turkey vultures were not a common sight in Acadia National Park but since the late 1980s more individuals are seen each year in the air over Mount Desert Island, especially over the mountain tops.

SAW-WHET OWL

The smallest of the owls regularly found in the park is the saw-whet owl (*Aegolius acadicus*). It is barely the size of your hand. This tiny owl has no ear tufts and when sitting it seems about the size of a fat sparrow. In flight they look bigger; their wingspan is about 20 inches. With a short fat body and the large wings the owl sometimes imparts a bat-like quality, especially when seen at dusk.

The voice of the saw-whet owl is most unusual and has been described as sounding like the "beeping" sound made by a big truck when it is backing up.

Although shy, and strictly nocturnal one may be seen resting in a thicket, and you might be allowed to get quite close. In spite of its tameness never touch one for they have sharp talons and are not as innocent as they appear. Despite its size, it is quite fierce and has been known to kill a mammal as large as a cottontail rabbit. It has great patience when hunting and will wait for hours for some prey it has seen briefly to reappear.

Look for these owls as you hike the park trails especially in woodlands along streams.

BARRED OWL

Barred owls (*Strix varia*) are very vocal, and campers sometimes fall asleep listening to two birds "talking" to each other through the night. The call has been described as *"Who cooks for you, Who cooks for you-all?"* with an emphasis on the *"you-all"* part. Barred owls call year-round but especially during courtship in February and March when pairs hoot a noisy, ardent owl duet.

This owl has no ear tufts and is best recognized by its dark eyes and large, rounded head, crosswise barring on the breast and lengthwise streaking on the belly; its back is spotted with white. It is the only large, brown-eyed owl in the East. Think of it as being almost as tall as the distance from your elbow to your finger tips (from 18 to 22 inches).

Barred owls nest in March, but they are not good nest builders and usually make use of an abandoned nest or tree cavity. If they do try on their own, the nest is so inexpertly constructed that the eggs often fall out or the young are injured. Although the female does most of the incubating, the male takes a turn at times, while the female drinks or bathes. During the incubation period, which lasts almost a month, the male brings food to his mate. After hatching, it's six weeks before the new little owls fly on their own. The bulk of this owl's diet is rats and mice.

Barred owls have been seen near Eagle Lake.

SNOWY OWL

If you visit in the winter months you might be lucky enough to see a snowy owl (*Nyctea scandiaca*). These large white owls appear along the shores, most often sitting on the ground, but sometimes on a rooftop. Hikers on the mountains in the park have found them sitting on the rocky summits. Individuals are reported each year especially on Sargent Mountain. Since they are not used to people they tend not to exhibit fear and may allow you to get quite close to them.

It has a round head, no ear tufts and appears neckless. Some birds may appear whiter than others. Most owls are night fliers but the snowy

owl is one of the day-time fliers. When in flight the snowy owl looks like a huge moth flying silently over the beach, salt marsh, or mountain slopes.

This owl is only seen on MDI and in the park during the winter when a few of these birds migrate south from the Arctic. Large migrations are cyclic and seem to depend on the availability of its prey.

MALLARD

This handsome duck with the iridescent dark green head is found most anywhere, for it readily adapts itself to civilization. It is the chief "puddle duck" found throughout the world. The mallard (*Anas platyrhynchos*) is a large duck strikingly marked with a green head and neck with a white collar, chestnut-red chest, and silvery gray body. Its middle and upper tail feathers curl upward giving an interesting effect.

Courtship may start as early as February with the male performing interesting courtship antics. He swims restlessly about, sidles up to a female, bobs his head in nervous jerks (so much so at times that the bill dips into the water), and displays his breast to win his lady. If all goes well with his amorous intentions the female begins to bow and accept him. When courtship is carried out on the wing it is another display worth watching as two or three males circle over a female sitting below. In rapid flight and with lots of loud quacking the males circle about until the female flies up and touches the male of her choice with her bill. They then fly off together.

These abundant ducks generally build their nests on the ground near any type of freshwater. The mother lines the nest with down and feathers from her breast. Mallard drakes usually take no interest in the family after the eggs are laid and gather in small flocks by themselves. The mother duck, however, is always alert and takes good care of her brood of eight or ten.

The mallards' menu is quite varied and the ducks do mankind a good service in consuming large quantities of mosquito larvae. Mallards will feed in stagnant pools where mosquitoes breed and eat thousands of them as well as drowning thousands more by stirring up the waters.

Although found elsewhere in the park, the very best place to see them in large numbers is in the small pond in front of the Seawall Dining Room, locally called Annabelle's Place, near the entrance to the Seawall section of the park on 102 A.

RUFFED GROUSE

The ruffed grouse (*Bonasa umbellus*) is a hardy woodland bird and can live very well through a Maine winter.

Hikers usually are first aware of this bird's presence when it seems to explode at their feet from behind the nearest bush or tree in a noisy, whirring flight. At other times you will see this red-brown or gray-brown chicken-like ground bird sitting in the branches of a tree eating buds. In the first warm days of spring you may find one taking a dust bath in a hollowed out saucer-shaped depression on a carriage road. They do this to rid themselves of feather lice.

The ruffed grouse is famous for its drumming, which is either a challenge to other males or an invitation to receptive females. They have been known to drum every month of the year, day or night, but the intensive drumming is done in early spring during late March and April. The act is actually performed on a well chosen, favorite log averaging about 20 inches wide and usually not less than 10 feet long. While drumming, the bird stands crosswise on the log, braces himself on his tail, and brings the wings forward and upward with quick strokes. He starts slowly at first, then increases in speed until the beats roll on and finally end in a rapid whirr. The source of the sound is often deceiving for it can be made a quarter of a mile away and sound as if only a hundred yards off.

It is quite possible to encounter a ruffed grouse anywhere in the wooded sections of the park. Be alert for them in a tree or walking stealthily through the underbrush.

The spruce grouse (*Dendragapus canadensis*) makes a sound similar to that of a ruffed grouse but not as loud nor as resonant. It is most often seen on the Wonderland Trail off 102 A near Seawall.

BLACK-BACKED WOODPECKER

The elusive and rare member of the woodpecker family to look for is the black-backed (*Picoides arcticus*) wood-pecker. Both sexes are recognized by the black back, wings and tail, but only the male has a yellow cap. This species has only three toes on each foot. Their voice has been described as sounding like a short, sharp "*cruck*" or "*crick*." Both sexes drum.

When feeding, these woodpeckers cling to dead and dying spruce trees where they very carefully flake away the scales of bark in their search for the larvae of wood boring beetles. The bird strikes the tree with a direct blow then, turning its head from side to side, strikes its beak slantingly into and under the bark and flakes it off. These foraging sites tend to be lower in live than dead trees, and more often in dead trees. The woodpecker makes good use of dense, low undergrowth and fallen, rotting logs.

This woodpecker normally breeds in the dense woods of Canada and migrates to MDI for the winter. As they work the trees they are unsuspicious and it is quite possible to walk up close to a bird and watch it work.

The best place to look is in the spruce woods of the park along the road leading to the Bass Harbor lighthouse.

DOWNY AND HAIRY WOODPECKER

Downy (*Picoides pubescens*) and hairy (*Picoides villosus*) woodpeckers are best seen at feeders, although you frequently may see them in the woods especially if you are sitting quietly.

In general appearance these two birds are very much alike and the only woodpeckers with a white back. Both are spotted and checkered with black and white and the males have a small red patch on the back of the head. Of the two, the commonly seen downy woodpecker is smaller (6 1/2 to 7 inches) and has a shorter, thinner bill. The hairy woodpecker is a little bigger (8 1/2 to 10 1/2 inches) and its bill seems a little large for the bird.

Downy Woodpecker

The voices of these look-alike woodpeckers are a bit different but you must listen carefully to notice it. The downy utters a rapid whinny of notes, descending in pitch. The hairy's similar sound is more run together. The little flat "*pick*" of the downy is not as sharp as the "*peek!*" of the hairy.

Drumming is a declaration of territorial claims and part of the bird's courtship. These woodpeckers favor certain drumming locations for their resonance, be it post, limb or the side of a building. The downy's drumming is a two-second unbroken roll, which makes the bird's head a blur. The drumming roll of the hairy is a bit shorter and louder.

They can be seen in woods all over the island. The best way to find one is to sit in one spot where there are both young and old trees and to listen for the tapping. After you have heard their tapping, follow the sound and you are likely to be able to get close enough to see the bird.

Hairy Woodpecker

WARBLERS

Warblers in the park are seen at their best in the spring, for they are then in their breeding plumages and more easily identified. Nests of 21 species have been found in the southwestern portion of the island over the past fifty years. Many arrive in the latter part of May to begin nest building.

The song of the yellow warbler is a musical "*sweet-sweet-sweet, sweeter-than-sweet.*" It is the only mostly yellow warbler with yellow spots—not white—on the tail. The male can be identified by the rust-colored streaks on his breast.

The lisping, dreamy "*zoo zee zoo zoo zee*" sound of the black-throated green warbler is easily recognized.

Yellow Warbler

This beautiful bird has a bright yellow face framed by a black throat, and has an olive-green crown and back. The female is less colorful but can still be recognized by her yellow face patch.

The parula warbler is the only bluish warbler with a yellow throat and breast. Its two white wing bars are also conspicuous. When viewing from underneath, look for a dark band crossing the yellow breast of the male bird. Females can be identified by the general blue and yellow coloring and white wing bars but the cross band on the breast will be quite indistinct or lacking altogether. The song of the parula is a buzzy trill which climbs the scale and ends with a sort of low pitched "*tup.*"

Ship Harbor and Wonderland are two good locations for observing warblers as well as along the road at the edge of the heath nearby. Also look near Sieur de Mont Springs and the Abbey Museum just off the Park Loop Road near Bar Harbor.

Trails through the Great Meadow adjacent to the Wild Flower Gardens of Acadia make it a good birding area, and it's easily accessible.

COMMON RAVEN

The sonorous call of the common raven (*Corvus corax*) often fills the air, and unless you see ravens and crows together it is sometimes quite difficult to distinguish them until they call. Ravens make a hoarse croak rather than the "*caw*" of a crow but they are also capable of making many different sounds, even imitating other birds and mammals they have heard.

In flight ravens look like large crows for they are all black and nearly twice as bulky as crows and usually show a wedge-shaped tail. Ravens have a hawk-like flight as they alternate flapping with soaring on their horizontal wings. They are fond of aerial acrobatics and will dive with closed wings and then suddenly turn over in the air. You are not "seeing things" if you should happen to witness a raven upside down overhead—a sight well worth watching!

Ravens nest in large forked trees in the forest as well as on sheltered rock ledges in the mountains or on the coast. Their breeding season begins about mid-April on MDI. They can be seen carrying twigs and sticks about as they build their nests. They line them first with grass tufts, leaves and moss, then with an inner lining of wool and hair. Both sexes build the nest; incubation is done by the female. During this period she is fed by the male. When the young hatch they are tended by both parents and are very vocal in their expressions of hunger. They leave the nest when they are five or six weeks old and the woods are noticeably more quiet.

Most of their food is taken from the ground—carrion, reptiles, young and wounded birds, eggs, insects and invertebrates. They also will take some vegetables and readily learn to eat human foods. They are excellent scavengers and hide any surplus food for later.

A good place to see ravens year-round is on Cadillac Mountain on the higher slopes. They are also found in areas of tall spruce woods.

RING-BILLED GULL

A gull you can see quite easily in the park is the ring-billed gull (*Larus delawarensis*). It is a little larger than a crow. It acts a great deal like a herring gull, but as its name implies, it has a dark ring around its bill rather than a red spot. Since this gull tends to be tame you most likely will be able to get a good look at its yellow feet. They are seen throughout the year in Acadia, and found on both fresh- and saltwater.

Ring-billed gulls are great insect eaters with a particular love for grasshoppers stirred up in a plowed field. As they fly, these birds seize the grasshoppers as easily as a swallow in pursuit of smaller insects. When food is discovered in water this gull floats down slowly or plunges downward and seizes the food without wetting its plumage.

These gulls rise neatly from the water, and can swim well. When alarmed they utter a shrill, piercing note of protest "*kree, kreeeee.*" They are also often noisy when feeding.

The ring-billed gull is highly gregarious and is usually seen in large flocks as well as associating with other species. The Thompson Island picnic area opposite the visitor's information center just after you cross the Trenton Bridge onto MDI is a good viewing area.

Summer visitors to the park may also see the smaller laughing gull (*Larus atricilla*), with its black head, gracefully flying along the shore. Its call is a "*haah-ha-ha-ha-ha*" and does sound like a laugh.

These gulls nest fifteen miles east of MDI, on Petit Manan Island, a part of the National Wildlife Refuge on the eastern Maine coast. They do not nest on MDI or in the park but from April through October the laughing gull can be seen along the Park Loop Road and in local harbors.

SO YOU WANT TO KNOW MORE?

Here is a list of organizations and places you might like to visit when you're in the area of Acadia National Park on a wildlife watching trip.

National Park Visitor Center

Route 3 in Hulls Cove. Ranger programs at Seawall and Blackwoods Campgrounds. Schedule of events are also listed in *Acadia Weekly*, a free publication. Birding Check List available here. For more information, call 207-288-3338.

Wild Flower Gardens of Acadia

At Sieur de Mont Springs off Park Loop Road. Nice display in natural habitat; recreations of plant life found in the Park. This is a good place to see local birds. A Nature Center is also located next to the gardens. For more information, call 207-288-3338.

Friends of Acadia

A private organization dedicated to the preservation of Acadia National Park. For "hands on" experiences in assisting the park and more information about the work of this group, call 207-288-3340.

Acadia Zoological Park

Route 3 in Trenton. Open May through October. Excellent opportunity to see local wildlife such as porcupines, foxes, bob cats, deer, moose, crows and ravens up close. For more information, call 207-667-3244.

Mount Desert Oceanariums

In Bar Harbor on Route 3 just after you come on the island. In South West Harbor on Clark Point Road next to Coast Guard Station. In Bar Harbor at 1 Harbor Place next to the Municipal Pier. For more information, call 207-244-7330.

Natural History Museum

Founded by naturalist Stanley O. Grierson. Turrets Bldg. College of the Atlantic. Open June through October. For more information, call 207-288-5015.

Birding Hot Line

For the latest bird information in the park and on the Island, call 207-244-4116.

Wendell Gilley Museum of Bird Carving

South West Harbor, corner of Main and Herrick Rd. Bird carvings, exhibits, lectures. For more information, call 207-244-7555.

Blagden Nature Preserve

On Indian Point Road in Town Hill on 102. Hiking trails. Guided nature hikes. For more information, call 207-288-3338.

Abbey Museum of Maine Indian Artifacts

It overlooks the Wild Gardens of Acadia and the Nature Center, located off Route 3 between the towns of Bar Harbor and Otter Creek. Open mid-May through mid-October. For more information, call 207-244-3519.

BIBLIOGRAPHY

Bent, Arthur Cleveland. *Life Histories of North American Diving Birds.* Dodd Mead and Company, 1946.

———. *Life Histories of North American Gulls and Terns.* Dodd, Mead and Company, 1947.

Book of North American Birds, Reader's Digest Association, Inc., 1990.

Butcher, Russell D. *Field Guide to Acadia National Park.* Readers Digest Press, 1977.

Clark, Neal. *Eastern Birds of Prey.* Thorndike Press, 1983.

Coffin, Tammis, editor. *The Rusticator's Journal.* Friends of Acadia, 1993.

Coman, Dale Rex. *The Native Mammals, Reptiles and Amphibians of Mount Desert Island.* University of Pennsylvania, 1972.

Eckert, Allan W. *The Owls of North America.* Weathervane Books, 1987.

———. *The Wading Birds of North America.* Weathervane Books, 1987.

Forbush, Edward Howe and May, John Richard. *A Natural History of American Birds of Eastern and Central North America.* Houghton Mifflin Co., 1939.

Forsyth, Adrian. *Mammals of the America North.* Camden House Pub., Ltd., 1985.

Godin, Alfred J. *Wild Mammals of New England.* The Johns Hopkins University Press, 1977.

Grierson, Ruth Gortner. *Nature Diary of Mount Desert Island.* Windswept House Publishers, 1993.

Hall, Henry Marion. *A Gathering of Shore Birds.* The Devin-Adair Company, 1960.

Hamilton Jr., William. *The Mammals of Eastern United States.* Comstock Publishing Co., Inc., 1943.

Harrison, Colin. *A Field Guide to Nests, Eggs and Nestlings of North American Birds.* Collins, 1978.

Katona, Steven K.; Rough, Valerie; and Richardson, David. *A Field Guide to the Whales, Porpoises and Seals of the Gulf of Maine and Eastern Canada.* Charles Scribner's Sons, 1983.

Kortright, Francis. *The Ducks, Geese and Swans of North America.* Stackpole Company and Wildlife Management Institute, 1942.

Lemon, Robert. *Our Amazing Birds.* Doubleday and Company, Inc., 1952.

Long, Ralph H. *Native Birds of MDI and Acadia National Park.* Beech Hill Pub. Co., 1987.

Peterson, Roger Tory. *A Field Guide to the Birds.* The Riverside Press, 1934.

Short, Lester L. *Woodpeckers of the World.* Delaware Museum of Natural History, 1982.

Stokes, Donald and Lillian. *A Guide to Animal Tracking and Behavior.* Little, Brown and Company, 1986.

———. *Guides to Bird Behavior, Vols I, II, and III.* Little, Brown and Company, 1989.

Tuttle, Merlin D. *America's Neighborhood Bats.* University of Texas Press, 1988.